Legends of Altai

BOOK 1

Chronicles of King Argoz and Princess Maya

Written by Paolo F. Tiberi

Published by Effective Life Strategies Pty Ltd
www.effectivelifestrategies.com

Copyright © 2010 by Paolo F. Tiberi All right reserved

No part of this book is to be reproduced by any mechanical, photographic, electronic process, or in the form of a phonographic recording. It may not be stored in any retrieval system, transmitted, and copied for public or private use without consent from the author – other than for *"fair use"* as brief quotations in the embodiment of articles or reviews.

The author of this book does not dispense medical advice or prescribe the use of any technique as a form of treatment for any physical, mental or emotional problem. The author has two intents with this book: 1) To offer a book with stories to open one's mind and heart so it may rekindle the inner fire contained within the soul. 2) To help individuals in their quest for spiritual well-being and developing a more fulfilled life.

A CIP catalog record for this book is
available from the Australian Library
Author: Tiberi, Paolo F.
Title: Chronicles of King Argoz, Prince Ultan and Princess Maya - written by Paolo F. Tiberi.
ISBN: 978-1-921851-10-0 (pbk.)
Series: Legends of Altai - Book 1
Audience: For primary school age and older
(Adults love the stories too!)

Contents

1. An Important Letter to Parents 05

2. How to get the best out of this book......................07

3. About Altai..11

4. The King and the Thief...13

5. King Argoz and the Wisdom of the Blue Violet....28

6. King Argoz and the Street Girl................................45

7. Princess Maya's Plan..65

8. Work-Book for Students..86

9. Coloring Book …..124

10. Teachers/Parents Reference Book......................128

11. Connect, share this book with others.................152

AN IMPORTANT LETTER TO PARENTS

Dear Parents,

We all come from different cultural backgrounds, religions, and belief systems. However, the stories in this book can easily be adapted to fit any personal viewpoint. I believe it is better to equip our children with some form of self-awareness, wisdom, and knowledge than none at all.

We live in a society where our children have been unconsciously trained to disassociate themselves from feelings of compassion, empathy, or guilt. False heroes found in most video games, television shows, internet and movies often set this silent training.

Many of our leaders have forgotten that you cannot have a functional, balanced and caring society without functional children, therefore they allow this silent training to be ever present.

In a society where instant gratification has replaced true labour and dedication, children have grown to expect everything immediately. They want instant soup instead of a finely brewed broth, even though the latter is more flavorsome and better for them.

It is sad that we have found ourselves living in a world where success is measured by how many "toys" one possesses. Kids are subtly and passively trained to desire materialistic things more and more, and never feel content.

We do have a way to step in and give our children positive guidance for a more enriching future.

Through your life, your words and actions and through the gifts (like this little book) you give your child, you have the ability to make a positive, profound choice for your child's life. You can become their beacon of light by teaching them to become loving, caring, and wiser beings. This is what the true gifts of life are about.

I ask you to help us change society one small child at the time through this little book of wisdom.

I hope that after having read these stories, you will feel that they are worth sharing.

How to get the best out of this book

This book is for both adults and children alike. Every person has the ability to learn valuable lessons when they open up their hearts and minds.

I grew up hearing great ancient stories and parables that have helped me with my own personal growth and life. It is my wish to share these stories with you in the hope that they will live in your heart. As you grow older I believe you will pass them on from generation to generation. Wisdom and a solid foundation in life are the gifts that will keep on giving.

There is no better opportunity to bond with your child than by sharing tales that intrigue them and invite questions on life. This will help them internalize the message, lesson, and wisdom for themselves. That internalization will create the seed of true self-awareness that all people need to prosper in their daily experiences.

The best way to absorb the benefits of this book is to slow down. Take time to savour each story. When you read them, make sure you listen to what the tale is telling you within the realms of not only your mind, but also your heart. We often forget how wise our hearts can be, too.

After you complete a story, there are a few questions you and your child could reflect upon:

* How did this story touch me?
* Did this tale awaken anything inside me?
* How could I use the message to positively affect or better my life and/or others?
* Is there any aspect of my life that needs the kind of understanding and healing addressed in the story?

It is impossible to read the tales in this book and not form a personal relationship with each one of them. Some of the stories may have a more profound effect on you than others, but the more you read them, the more you will find the different levels of meaning within each one.

Since people all react differently to the messages in these tales, they can become great tools to start communication with those around you. Some of you may want to laugh or cry. Others will simply be touched by the message of the story. In the end, there is neither a right nor wrong reaction. Rather, there is an opportunity to learn about your true self and open up the doors to discussions about life and its choices with your children, friends, or family.

Let each one of these stories flow through your mind, heart and self freely. Contemplate on the messages learned, and if you can feel that it has moved you, make sure to share it with others.

Everyone can benefit from your self-realization and perhaps inspire others to emulate the messages learnt. You have the unlimited potential to reach out and touch somebody, either by calling them, emailing them, or writing a letter to let them know that you have learned or have been reminded of something amazing.

Since the goal is for every child to relate to these stories with a universal message, the word "God" has been changed to "The Great One" to make it easier to accept.

FREE GIFTS IN THIS BOOK:
1. Parent/Teacher & Student Workbook for story 1.
2. A coloring book, containing all of the main characters.

To see availability of Book 2, 3 and 4 please visit:

www.legendsofaltai.com

About Altai

The Altai Mountains are one of the most serene, secluded and beautiful locations on Earth. They remain that way because of their exclusiveness and limited accessibility.

The name Altai has origins from the word Altan; which means golden mountains in the Mongolian dialect. Altai lies securely in a mountain range in central Asia that stretches for 2,000 kilometers and forms a natural border between Russia, China, Mongolia and Kazakhstan.

There has never been another place like Altai since anyone can remember; where extraordinary events, spirituality, and mysticism meet common life. A land that some people believe is a doorway between heaven and earth attracting seekers of spiritual enlightenment into its realm for countless millennia.

For more information on the mystical place called Altai, please visit: www.legendsofaltai.com

1. The King and the Thief

Once upon a time there lived a wise King. He was called Argoz the Great, and he was a strong, powerful and just ruler. It had not always been that way.

When Argoz was still but a prince, he cared only for himself. He ignored his people and thought they were beneath him. His actions showed that he thought their only purpose was to serve him. His greatest pleasure was to gratify his senses with luxury and beauty.

He would throw lavish banquets and parties with platters of fruit, cheeses, and satisfying foods. He made sure that his palace grounds were surrounded by beautiful gardens that had fragrant flowers always in bloom and delicious fruit just a touch away. Argoz' rooms were adorned with treasures and trinkets.

When Argoz' father, King Amado, passed away, it was no surprise to the Kingdom that life changed drastically. What was once bountiful was now scarce. There were many taxes imposed on his people.

The once loyal Kingdom began to struggle. They could not support the lavish lifestyle of King Argoz.

If anybody was caught not paying their taxes, they were sent to prison. There were no excuses that were acceptable. A great drought came one year and ruined all the crops that provided food for King Argoz' Kingdom. People began to starve, and the burdened workers in the Kingdom did not have enough money to pay for taxes.

Without food, the Kingdom was weak. People became desperate and started to steal food. They could no longer pay their taxes, so they hid in fear. All of this was unknown to the selfish King.

The young King was only concerned with his welfare. His advisors reassured him with the words he wanted to hear. They spoke of how great he was and let him know that his laws were fair and certainly justified. As a vain young man who wanted to be loved, King Argoz did not understand why his people loathed him. They should adore him like they loved his father. The Kingdom continued to disobey his commands.

His advisors continued to be cowards and not speak the truth.

The Kingdom was being destroyed and could not keep going. Taxation and starvation were the true rulers of the Kingdom, not King Argoz.

After King Argoz could bear no more, he decided to go seek the truth himself. He could not stand the thought of not being adored by his people.

He dressed up in peasant clothes like what his servants wore and snuck out the back gate of his palace's protective walls. As he went out into the village, he felt fear. People were not happy and his name was spoken with a great, sorrowful tone. He did not understand.

Aside from hunting expeditions, the young King Argoz had never been allowed to leave the secure walls of his palace. The palace was his life, and it was designed to provide everything that King Argoz needed to live a life worthy of a young King. As he looked around and wandered the streets, he felt as if he was living a nightmare. His eyes had never seen such emotions, and he had never experienced people not backing away as he approached. Dressed as a villager in his Kingdom, he was treated like everyone else. Although King Argoz had dressed in disguise, his ego was bruised by the fact that nobody recognized him and paid him respect.

Following closely behind King Argoz were his most loyal guards. They also were dressed like the villagers and nobody realized who they were. They mingled with people upon their King's orders and tried to seek the answers the young King sought. They were all too cowardly to speak the truth to King Argoz.

As he walked through the trodden dirt streets of his Kingdom, King Argoz noticed hard-working people. His instincts told him to pay attention to one man in particular. This man walked by a vegetable stand and grabbed some potatoes and sweet fruits.

He snuck them into his sack while the shop owner was talking with another man. As swiftly as his hand had grabbed what was not his, he walked away.

His eyes darted from left to right and he hugged the sack close to his chest, as if it was his most worldly possession.

The King and his guards kept their eyes on this man. He walked down alleys and entered into a lone wooden door in the darkest part of the alley. They followed close behind. The King had commanded his loyal guardsmen to use their authority and arrest this man. Who was he to steal food that would feed the King or pay taxes to him? It was treason and could not be tolerated.

After the thief entered his home at the end of the alley, the King and his troops barged through the wooden door. It crumbled as if it had been made of sawdust. The open air made the small fire flame up to the chimney. Smoke billowed up the chimney-stack and puffed into the small home. They found themselves standing in the middle of a small circular room, a room that was smaller than the King's lowest servant's chambers.

Closely laid around the small open fireplace were five woven floor mats for sleeping. In the center of the room was a small table with one small loaf of bread, two carrots, and an apple.

This was something that the King had never seen before. He slowly digested the scene. It was as foul as rotten food. Slowly, the young King turned his head to the other side of the hut. The people before him paid him no attention. The thief was hunched over somebody. To his side were a wife and two young daughters. They all looked worried about what was before them and were not fazed by the door being burst open. Their hearts and minds were focused on the small mat on the floor. The King noticed a small child lying there. You could see the sweat beads glistening on his smooth young forehead. He was pale and as fragile as a new blossom in a violent storm.

Tears stung the young King's eyes. This was something new to him. He could feel his skin prickling with angst. He didn't know what to do. This family before him showed love and compassion. Yet, they had nothing beautiful around them. It didn't appear they had enough to feed themselves. How could they live so sadly? The young King Argoz felt his throat closing up. As much as he wanted to, he could not turn away. The image was burnt in his mind and eyes. King Argoz' stomach churned violently. He felt consuming guilt and his heart wept with sorrow. He could not believe that anybody in his Kingdom lived so humbly. Was he not a good just King?

The King tried to regain his composure. Just as he was about to speak, one of his guards revealed their Regal Seal. They demanded that the family kneel before the King. For the first time, the family focused on the strangers in their small room. Their faces were stricken with horror. The family knelt as swiftly as possible and bowed their heads to the ground.

They wept silently. They were so ashamed of their actions and begged for mercy and forgiveness from the young King.

One of the guards demanded answers. "Don't you know that stealing in this Kingdom is punishable with imprisonment?" The thief nodded his head and looked down. The unseen weight on his shoulders was clearly visible in his weariness.

The guard had no patience or compassion. "Speak villager, why would you do such a thing?"

The thief's eyes were tired and worn. He looked up at the King and said, "Please forgive me, my King. I have no food to feed my family and my son is sick. We have no money to pay the village doctor or money to pay taxes. I was going to sell what I stole for money to buy medicine for my son. Please great King, show us some mercy, spare our lives and forgive us. I will do what I must to pay it back, plus more."

The King swallowed hard. He had never had a decision to make on his own. King Argoz became aware that his advisors had always made his decisions for him. He had never cared before because his life was lavish and good. The young King looked around the hut for what seemed like an eternity. He wondered what he would do in this humble villager's situation. His eyes betrayed him and began to sob. The King's knees grew weak and he collapsed to the ground. The King looked like a vulnerable, broken man. He also felt like one. He had finally seen the world through someone else's eyes. His guards looked down at him completely bewildered and unsure of what to do.

After time, the burden of the King's heart lifted and his sobbing stopped. He regained his composure. He slowly rose from the ground and turned to his chief guard. He placed his left hand on the chief guard's shoulder and calmly said, "Take this family to the palace now. Bathe them, feed them well, and let the young child be attended to by the Royal Physician. They shall stay in one of the guest rooms tonight. New arrangements will be made tomorrow. This is my command."

Word of King Argoz' kind deed spread through the Kingdom rapidly. It was an instant source of inspiration and joy for people who were so tired from their burdens. Within the next few days, the King opened the palace food reserve to feed his people. He saw that his unjust taxes could be reduced. The lavish lifestyle of the young King Argoz was replaced by a life devoted to his people. Little by little, the entire Kingdom began to flourish again.

It was through those times of growth that a once selfish man became known as "Argoz the Great."

The greatest part of this young King was that the best was yet to come.

2. King Argoz and the Wisdom of the Blue Violet

After the event in the villager's hut, the King's desire to help others started to grow. Like all great men, he responded to the opening of his heart and wanted to learn more. He invited the greatest teachers from all over the world to the Kingdom. They were welcomed and treated with great honour.

King Argoz invited them to freely share their knowledge and wisdom with both him and his people.

These great teachers taught everybody about the things they could use to make a more prosperous life for themselves. Some taught about herbs and remedies for common ailments or fever. Others shared wisdom about growing crops and treating the valuable land with respect. There were also teachers who understood mathematics, astronomy, pursuits of happiness, and true inner serenity. All the teachers brought great value and wisdom to the Kingdom. Some came in regal caravans, others arrived by foot, but they all came with one purpose in mind – to share their teachings with the villagers in the Kingdom.

King Argoz was fascinated by everything he was learning and the ways of these most welcome foreigners. They embraced every question and curiosity that was expressed. The teachers said that a thirst for knowledge and information was healthy and part of humankind's greater purpose. One day while discussing life with a great teacher, the King expressed a desire: "I wish I could understand life more fully. I want to understand why some people and living things are born into very hard conditions, while others' lives are full of peace and bountifulness."

The Great Teacher said, "Dear King, indeed you have acted with wisdom and generosity towards your people. If what you really desire is true wisdom, I will grant your wish. I will make it so you hear and understand the true plans behind the Great One's creation. This new skill will enable you to appreciate the workings of life. Are you sure of this desire, King Argoz?"

"I am sure, Great Teacher. I thirst for this knowledge." Then, the Great Teacher touched the King gently on his forehead.

A jolt of energy surged through the King and travelled deep within him. The King fainted.

Upon regaining consciousness, the King could hear the Great Teacher's welcoming voice. His tone was calm and soothing. "Look at this great and mighty oak tree in front of us. Listen closely. What do you hear, my King?"

The King slowly arose. He focused his eyes, which were still heavy from the jolt of energy, and tried to open his ears to what the great oak tree was saying. He started to grow impatient. He heard nothing at all. "This is not working Great Teacher. I hear nothing at all."

"Listen not with your ears, but with the deepest part of yourself, King Argoz. Close your eyes, breathe deeply, and try to create a space of silence within you. You may have never visited this place before, but you will know it once you find it."

The King closed his eyes and took a deep breath. He cleared his mind. He started to feel this new spot within him open up. To his great surprise he heard a voice coming from the tree. "I am very glad that you can hear my voice, Great King," said the tree.

"Thank you for talking to me, mighty oak tree."

The King smiled and embraced the Great Teacher. "This has been a most amazing experience. Will I learn more?"

"You will," the teacher responded.

Many days passed by. The King enjoyed spending more time in his garden and the lush forest. He listened to the voices of the trees and flowers. He started to develop a deeper understanding of how everything on earth was connected. The world was unfolding in front of his very eyes and his mind opened up to how this world was created from the magnificent dreams of God, The Great One.

King Argoz was walking through his splendid garden one sunny day. As he rounded the twisting path, he could hear weeping. He looked closer and found the source. It was a rose. He gently knelt down to be closer to the weeping rose. "Why are you crying, dear rose?"

"My dear King, I cry because the Great One saw fit to make me with thorns. When people touch me, they experience pain and not joy. They are afraid of me. It is so much to bear and it makes me very sad. Why can I not be beautiful like a multi colored orchid? They have no thorns and they hurt nobody." The sad rose could not stop sobbing.

The King was perplexed. As he thought of ways he could help, he gently caressed the rose, trying to bring her comfort. He had no solutions. "Rose, I shall think of how I can help you. I wish you to be happy, for I think you are beautiful. The Great One does not create without a purpose. You do have a purpose."

"Will you help me find my purpose, King Argoz?"

The King agreed to help and started on his way back to the palace. Again, he heard crying. This time he noticed that it was an orchid.
"Tell me orchid, why are you crying?"

"Because I have no beautiful scent that people are inspired to inhale. Nobody looks at me, because I have no essence for them to rejoice in. If only I was a rose, then people would love me and smell my wonderful fragrant petals. That is why I am crying."

The King tried to provide comfort to the orchid, but the crying did not stop. "You are a wonderful gift for people to behold, dear orchid. Please do not be sad. Let me ponder on how I can best help you. I will be back."

As the King approached the inner courtyard of his palace, he noticed two tall cypress trees grumbling at each other. They were angry and their branches were swiftly moving back and forth. The King walked up to them. "What is bothering you, majestic trees?"

"Oh Great King, we are upset because we are not as beautiful as the orchid. Nor do we have the fragrant scent of a rose. We are not appreciated and most do not realize we are here unless they seek shade."

"There is so much sadness and misery on the palace grounds today. I believe you two are most magnificent and amazing.

I find you deeply rooted in this world. Let me ponder this and come back to visit."

The King was deeply perplexed and saddened. He sat on the steps of the palace and contemplated what he could do to help the beautiful rose, orchid, and cypress trees. To the King's side was a small bush of blue violet. It spread out and carpeted the floor. It reached all the way to the most remote spots of his beautiful garden. In the distance was a spot he had never noticed before. Another bush of blue violet was glowing with happiness and singing songs of praise. After the sorrowful nature of the King's walk, he was curious about why this bush was celebrating.

The King stood up and walked towards the small bush of blue violet bush and asked, "Little blue violet, why are you so happy?"

"Dear King, I am celebrating the joy of being myself!" exclaimed the blue violet bush.

"When the Great One created me, great thought was put into how my essence could best express its divine vision. I was created with these little blue violet flowers. They were meant to be this color; not yellow, red, or any other color. The Great One wished not for me to be tall with a majestic trunk. No, my King, it envisioned me as a little one, a plant that could spread and cover the ground with a lovely carpet of green and blue. When the Great One selected my scent, it was made similar to chocolate. This is because chocolate would best fit my exuberant personality," the bush spoke merrily and glowed with true happiness.

Blue violet continued, "My King, the Great One knows that the purpose of one's life is not how we look, smell, or feel. It does not even matter what our situation or experiences are. What counts with the Great One is that we know the purpose of life."

The King stood silently, absorbing the words of the wise blue violet. "In its wisdom, the Great One created the best body, smell, and look for me as a spirit. This has allowed me to experience the lessons I need to learn. The best way I can accomplish this is by embracing who I am and knowing that it is part of the plan. In this part of my journey, I am a blue violet bush."

"You are much attuned to your purpose, blue violet," King Argoz said.

"If the Great One had decided that I was to be born differently, it would be because it's my destiny, and would have brought me different life lessons. My body and current form is simply a garment used to learn the life lesson, nothing more. Only I can allow me to learn. Nobody else can. I have noticed that some plants might want to be taller or perhaps stronger, some wish for dazzling and beautiful colors or strength. They wish for everything but what the Great One has given them. Some may view me as small, weak, or even ugly… I don't mind. I know this is the perfect body form for me to express myself."

"How have you come to know so much? Many men would love to have this knowledge for a more peaceful existence," the King asked.

"I have listened, grown, and opened up my consciousness. Therefore, my King, I am fulfilled in being what I am. I am grateful for the life I was given to express the vision the Great One had for me. I have been given the gift of life. This life offers great opportunities. This is why I am happy and why I do not have any desire to be something else."

The King asked, "Blue violet, what would you say to all of the Great One's creations that are so unhappy about what they are?"

"I would let them know that they are more than their physical appearance, personality, and character. I'd remind them that they were created by the Great One and each one has a valuable lesson to learn from being just the way they are," blue violet said. "They should embrace their uniqueness and discover their purpose; for all of us matter. It is very important to show love and feel loved. That is how you reach understanding and see how you fit into the Great One's plan. Without each of us, the plan would be incomplete. Just as eagles need to fly, dolphins need to swim, and cheetah need to run – you need to do what you were intended to do with pride. We all have gifts that make us uniquely beautiful and perfect."

The King smiled at the wise blue violet. Blue violet continued, "Focus on your talents and true life purpose to discover your path in life.

When you focus on what you do not have you will not grow strong and healthy. If you are unsure of what your life's purpose is and haven't discovered your talents, you need to look deeper within you. Look at what you are passionate about and what gives you a warm feeling in your heart. That is where you'll find your answers."

The King sat down. Tears shone brightly in his eyes. He now realized the meaning of life and why everything must be different. Everything had its place, role and form as the Great One saw fit.

He also realised that challenges we face, bring strength and wisdom. We all fit in a special, often hidden plan.

King Argoz was excited to share what he had learned with the rose, orchid, and the cypress trees.

3. King Argoz and the Street Girl

The experience in the garden, the teachings of wise men, and his experience on the mountain top had a profound effect on King Argoz.

He saw how important it was to make a difference in people's lives. In particular, the great King wanted to help the people of his Kingdom.

One nice afternoon, King Argoz decided to dress in normal attire and walk through the market. He had done that only once before as a prince and it was a most useful day. The King wanted to make sure that his people were doing well with their businesses and that the market was a lively place for both comradeship and commerce.

The King camouflaged himself under a merchant robe and wore a fake beard and wig. He observed a small girl, perhaps seven years of age, scavenging for food in the streets of the market.

Her wide curious eyes would look at the rich people eating their fares and patiently wait for them to discard what they considered scraps. For this small girl, those scraps were her next meal and she cherished every one of them.

The King looked at the child. His guard noticed this gesture and asked, "What do you want to do, my Lord?"

"I don't want to make myself known, however, a street child is everyone's child. That means that everyone should feel responsible for her well-being and not accept her living in such conditions. Guard, you must try to find some loving parents who can take care of that little one. We must organise someone to look for these children of the street and start taking care of them. Meanwhile, let's try to give her some food," the King said.

King Argoz approached the little one and tried to speak with her. The presence of the two men approaching the little girl scared her. She ran away and hid in an alley off the street. This disturbed the King, but he didn't forget it. The next day the King was more prepared. He approached the market carrying a nice loaf of bread and some sweets.

The King addressed his guard. "Stay nearby, but not too close."

The dirty little street child looked up at the man slowly approaching her. She could see his beautiful green eyes very clearly. Her eyes could not help but watch the food that he held in his hands. The King left the food on a small rock bench close to a food stall, and slowly moved away.

The girl looked at the man. He smiled and signalled that it was ok for her to take the food. She gave a quick smile. Then she quickly grabbed the food and started to head away. The owner of the food stand noticed her and believed that she was stealing the food. He yelled out loudly. "Thief, thief!"

The guards patrolling the market rushed towards the poor little girl and grabbed her by her arm. The food fell to the ground.

The man from the food stand rushed over. "She stole this food from that man!" he yelled.

Now, none of the people in the market could recognise that the man in front of them was their King. His false beard and robe lead everybody to believe that he was just a merchant.

The little girl was terrified. Her eyes were wild with fear and tears .

"No, my dear friends, she has not stolen anything. I placed all of this food and sweets on the rock bench for her to take," King Argoz said. He swiftly approached the little girl, the guards, and the confused stall merchant.

"Why would you do such a thing for a beggar?" the merchant asked.

"Well, she has not asked me for anything. I just don't want her to eat off the street. No person deserves that, so please let her go," replied Argoz. He directed his request directly to the guards.

"I guess if there is no wrong doing, we do not have any issue with this little girl," said one of the guards.

He let the little girl go.

The little girl picked up the bundle of wrapped bread and sweets and sat down on the stone bench.

She ate the food as if she had not eaten anything for days.

King Argoz bent down so he could be on the same eye level as the little girl. He observed the scene. He had his guard organise more food for the little girl. They placed it in a bag and handed it to her. The King smiled and said, "See you tomorrow, little one. This bag should be enough for tonight and tomorrow morning."

The little girl smiled. She could tell that she could trust this odd-looking man with the brilliant green eyes. The man continued to return day after day for a week. On the eighth day, when the little girl saw the man arrive with more food, she ran to him and gave him her hand without any hesitation.

The King smiled. He was happy that the girl finally felt that his intentions were pure and his desire to help her was sincere. "What's your name, little one?"

"Little girl."

The King smiled. "That is what I call you. Can you tell me your real name?"

"I like little girl," she answered

"Do you mind if I find a pretty name for you?" the King asked.

"I would love one."

"Do you have parents?" asked the King.

"No sir. I have no parents. All I remember is being left here at the market one day by a woman. That was about a two and a half years ago," the little girl clearly expressed her sadness at the memory of that moment.

"Ok, little one, let's not talk about sad things. Let me get you some yummy food!" The King felt very sad and wanted to change the topic to bring cheer to the little girl.

The King and the little girl walked to one of the food stalls.

The people there were used to seeing them. The stall owner said, "I have seen this girl for the last year. She grabs food in the streets, but I never heard her say a word."

The stall owner smiled at them and so did the cart vendor close by. They could sense that the man really cared for this little girl.

"What would you like?" the King asked the little girl.

The little girl pointed at some of the food in the stall. The King tried to pay the stall owner for the food. As the King handed over the money, the stall owner stopped him. "I don't want any money from you. I will try to help this child and feed her whenever I can at no charge." The stall owner smiled at the little girl. The little girl gave him a wondrous, beautiful smile and ran off. The man kept his smile and went back to work.

The next morning on the way to the market the little one was waiting. She was hoping that the nice man would return. He did and this time he was not alone. The King, still clothed as a merchant, brought a nice large woman with him. She had a wooden panel, soap, a nice dress, and towels.

The King grabbed her small hand and laughed. "Would you like lunch again?" The little girl nodded. "Do you like the name Maya?" the King asked.

"What does Maya mean?" asked the little girl

"It means 'brave warrior' in some cultures, and 'beautiful girl' in others," responded the King

"I like it. I am Maya!" replied the little girl. She jumped up and down with excitement. She really liked her new name. This pleased the King and he could feel a lump in his throat.

"I have another small surprise for you," the King said. He had a cheeky smile upon his face and could not wait. "I have a beautiful dress for you to wear so that you can look like a real princess. Before you can wear it we have to clean you up a bit. Would that be okay?"

The little girl eagerly agreed. Her smile was bright and her thanks were sincere.

The King had arranged for the large plump woman to give Maya a quick bath near the park, where a panel would shield them from public view. He knew that it may be difficult to take her to a house for a proper bath, but this would be a good opportunity to help her out a little bit.

The round woman soaped Maya up and washed her with water. She wiggled the whole time but you could tell by the laughter on her face that she loved having someone care for her.

"Look Maya, the nice man brought this beautiful little dress for you.

You truly are going to love it," the lady said.

She dried her off with a towel. Maya's face was shining brightly as she looked at the beautiful dress. She thought it was the most beautiful dress in the world. A half hour had passed and the little girl came out. She truly looked like a little princess. Her beautiful blond curly hair whispered in the wind and no longer matted down. Her green eyes sparkled like shining emeralds sitting in the midday sun.

As the King waited for the last touches, he had not noticed that a small crowd had gathered around. King Argoz looked up into the beaming faces of men, women, and other children. The stall owner was also present. The little girl looked directly at the kind man and said, "Thank you, no one has ever done something like this for me. Thank You."

"You're welcome, Maya. It is ok and all will be fine," the King whispered in her ear.

One man observed the gestures of this bearded, robed man. He was moved and could not help but wonder. He asked, "Why are you doing so much for this child?"

It did not take the King long to respond, for he knew what was right. "We were all children at one time. One day we might become parents if we are not already one. Any lost child, with no relatives, belongs to all of us. It is our responsibility as a community to ensure that they are provided for and know that they matter. Every person in this Kingdom is a part of a family. No one should be left behind. Didn't the King go to the mountain to try to save his son? Isn't his son now recovering?"

"Yes, but that was his son. Who would do this for a beggar, a street child?" asked another man.

King Argoz smiled, his eyes sparkling.

A stall owner close by began to make some connections. He spoke in a half whisper because he was saying it to himself as well as whoever would listen, "Someone who truly cares, someone who wants to help and be of service to those in need." He looked at the man before him.

"I will make her clothes," offered a dressmaker.

"I will give her books and help educate her," a teacher said.

"I will give her food, as I had promised," the food stall owner added.

"I will provide her shoes," said the shoemaker.

"I will be her friend," said a small girl. She was about the same age and ran to grab her hand. She had a big smile and was set to play with her new friend.

These acts of kindness started to spread around the Kingdom. It was as if a miracle was happening right before people's eyes. A community of strangers united for a common purpose. They all felt so happy, content and their hearts were overflowing with the rewards that the love and kindness brought them.

Maya realised that this kind man might not be in her future any longer, so she turned to him and asked, "But you…what about you?"

The King embraced the child and said, "I will always be in your life, and you will always be my little girl, little Maya. Tell me what would you like more than anything else?"

"I would like to have a family that cares about me like you do. I would like you to be my father," sweet little Maya said. She looked at him honestly and the King was nearly in tears. He regained his composure and responded. "Then so it will be."

The little girl's eyes sparkled with joy. She was in such an excited frenzy that she jumped into the King's arms and began to cry. He hugged little Maya mightily. After a bit of time, the King looked up at the crowd. Everybody was smiling and crying.

"I want us all to celebrate this magnificent occasion. Therefore you are all invited to come to the Royal Palace this weekend for a celebration of community and spirit. Your generosity and sincere desire to help this little girl will be rewarded. Even if your hearts seek no rewards."

"But that's the King's palace. We cannot go there without an invitation," the food stall owner responded with confusion.

"So it is. Consider yourselves officially invited," King Argoz proclaimed. He had a small smile upon his face and reached up to remove his fake beard. Then he took off his top garment and revealed the royal vest, then the royal seal. The crowd was stunned. King Argoz' guard was still a few feet away. He moved forward and removed his disguise to reveal his royal guard's uniform.

The guard yelled out, "Bow citizens of the Kingdom, for you are in the presence of your King!" His voice sounded like thunder and it echoed through the market place. Everyone bowed, including little Maya.

"Rise, beautiful people," responded the King.

"Please know that everyone matters in our Kingdom and that every person counts. Today all of you showed that to me. I am proud that the people in my Kingdom care and are willing to make a difference. For that, I thank you. I hope to see you all this Sunday at the palace."

The crowd was speechless. They all nodded in awe. That Sunday little Maya became a princess, gained a brother, and discovered a circle of friends that truly cared. And on that day, the villagers and citizens of the Kingdom of Altai realised that miracles can happen to anyone and that when people truly care, everything is possible.

4. Princess Maya's Plan

Maya was a very smart young girl. Within a few months, she learned how to read and her desire for knowledge grew with each passing day. Her brother, Ultan, was twelve years old, and they both liked to share adventures and stories about great Kings, wizards, healers, and teachers. They certainly always looked forward to when a wise man would come to visit the court.

Everyone noticed that Maya was different and had a very special gift. She remembered every person's name in the castle and everyone's personal stories. Also, she had the most wonderful ability to make each and every person know that they were truly important.

In fact, every time one of the servants would tend to her room, she would stop them, look them in the eyes and say something like, "Maria, I thank you for tidying this room so well. I love how you always are so attentive and how you pay attention to even the tiniest of details. I really appreciate that. Thank you."

One of Maya's favourite things to do was go into the palace kitchen and speak with the chefs, cooks, and even the servants as they washed the dishes. Once again, she would stop them, look them in the eyes, and say, "Abenzio, Arland, Maralek, I truly appreciate your efforts. You always look for the freshest ingredients and the best recipes for us. We are truly honoured to get to feast on your creations. I always love meal times."

Then Maya looked at the servants washing the dishes stopped, and said, "Conall, Kimball, I am always so impressed with how clean the dishes are.

There is always a beautiful smell to them. What do you use?"

"Milady, we use white vinegar, water, soap, and lemon juice," said the servant.

"That's great. And how is your wife doing, Kimball?," continued Maya

"She is getting better, Milady. Thank you for asking," Kimball replied appreciatively.

One day Ultan and Maya spoke about ways to improve the Kingdom. After much thinking, they came up with a few great ideas. Maya began, "When father came and found me, he said something very important. Something that I will never forget. He said, 'Everyone matters, every person in this Kingdom is part of a family. No one should be left behind. Everyone, no matter who they are can make a difference.' That statement made all the difference in my life, and I believe it could in other people's lives too."

Maya continued, "When people do not feel special enough, they often end up feeling alone. They start to feel like their efforts go unnoticed. I have realized that when I compliment people, they do a better job, they feel prouder and feel that their life has a purpose."

"That's very true," said Ultan. "So how do we make people feel more appreciated and special?"

"We can start a small revolution of recognition!" exclaimed Maya. She was very excited at the thought and began to create a plan.

"What do you mean?" Ultan asked.

"Ultan, if I recognise the hard work of one person and then that person feels better and feels proud, they will go home feeling happy and content. That could make them want to do the same thing for their wife, husband, or children. Then they will feel good, too. They will then spread this kindness to those they see. Before you know it, this Kingdom and perhaps the world will be a better place." Maya was so confident in her idea and had a big smile on her face.

"We are so young, you are just eight years old. Do you truly think we can change the world?" questioned Ultan.

"Yes, our age and the size of the job does not matter, it's the intention that counts. Look how many people were willing to help me once father started to help. They didn't even know that he was the King. Father said that the first step of any idea is to actually start the journey. He also said that even the longest journey starts with a simple intention. He believes that the journey is more important than the destination itself! I do, too!," Maya explained.

"Hmm, true, true. You are right, but how do we test your strategy? I am sure it works, but we must find a way to test it."

"Oh, you boys like to test everything!" Maya laughed. She and Ultan laughed a lot when they were together.

"Well, I thought about creating a potion," Maya said. She had a twinkle in her eye.

"But you don't know how to prepare a potion," Ultan replied.

"Silly, it is not a potion developed from medicine. It is just a make-believe potion made from water and food coloring!"

"Ah, a placebo!" yelled Ultan.

"What's a placebo?"

"It is a fake medicine. People think that what you are giving them is like medicine, but in reality it is just colored water with a flavoring of sugar in it." Ultan explained.

"Yes, we can use a placebo for our potion. I like that a lot!"

"And how are you going to use this potion?" asked Ultan

"Well, Conall, one of the servants who washes the dishes, is quite old and has been married to his wife for more than 25 years. When I am in the kitchen sometimes I hear him calling his wife nasty names."

"Like what?" Ultan asked. He couldn't help but be intrigued by Maya's words.

"Usually silly things like, 'That old cow cannot appreciate all the work I do here in the kitchen. She does not even clean the house; all she does is spend, spend, spend', you know…awful things like that."

"Ok, so how do you intend to save their marriage with your magical potion?"

"Well, it is not really physical magic because the magic happens in the mind. This potion is all about changing someone's attitude and belief system or altering their state of mind."

"You see, all people live their lives based on the beliefs they have within themselves. These beliefs then define their attitude, how they see the world and react to people or situations. So if someone wants to have a completely different experience in their life, they must first change their belief." Maya indicated.

"I like it Maya. Ok, so how are you going to apply this plan with Conall?"

"Come with me and I will show you!" exclaimed Maya. As they walked towards the kitchen, she showed Ultan an electric blue liquid sealed inside a small glass tube.

Maya smiled and whispered cheekily, "Placebo." Ultan and Maya headed towards the kitchen and as usual, Maya stopped to congratulate everyone for their great work. She reached the area where the dishes were being washed and asked Conall if she could have a word with him in private.

"How can I be of service, milady?" asked Conall.

"It is not what you can do for us, dear Conall. But rather, what we can do for you." Maya replied respectfully.

Conall listened intently.

"You know we always get very interesting gifts at court....

Especially from great healers and wise men"

"Yes milady" you do

"Well...." Maya removed the glass flask with the beautiful color from behind her back as she spoke.

"This flask contains a very special, unique potion that can bring out the best that any woman has within herself. She would transform into a beautiful angel both beautiful inside and out. She would be a woman whom any man would be blessed with."

A long silence followed, but Conall still listened.

"This gift is for you, Conall. I have decided to give it to you!"

Conall cried, "Milady, I am not worthy of such a gift."

"Maybe not yet, but an angel needs someone to take special care of her. The only way the transformation can happen is if every day, in every possible way, you make this angel feel special, accepted, appreciated and make her feel like she is a true goddess.

When you do these things, this will activate the magic potion and transform your wife into an angel. You are worthy of this gift and taking care of the angel is just as important as the potion. Do you understand?" asked Maya.

"I do," Conall replied. "How can I repay you? This is so much to give."

"No need. You and your wife's happiness is my reward," said Maya. She smiled tenderly.

"How do I give her the potion?" asked the man.

"Here are two silver coins. Go and buy her favourite wine. Pour a glass for her and add the potion into it. It might taste a bit fruity. The changes will happen almost immediately. It might take a few months for the full transformation to take place."

"I am so grateful, but I still don't understand why you would choose me for this."

"Because you need it more than any other person I know. Like my father said, every person has a purpose and every person is important. No matter what they decide to do, they have a choice to do the right things to show other people that they matter. You are worthy of this gift, and it will make your relationship with your wife and life special until the end of your days!"

They embraced.

"Please keep me informed on your wife's transformation, Conall," said Maya, smiling tenderly.

"I will," replied Conall with glee.

Ultan and Maya left Conall in the kitchen. He was looking at the blue glass tube in awe. That night the old dishwasher went home a different man. He looked at his wife in a new way. She noticed him watching her and felt a bit uncomfortable. She was not used to that kind of attention.

"Are you drunk?" she asked sarcastically.

"No, but maybe we will both be later. I bought your favourite wine to celebrate the day I first met you. I am so happy that you are in my life and I am thankful for all you have done for me all these years," he answered.

She was stunned and speechless. Her plump cheeks turned rosy from blushing. She ran to the bathroom and made sure her hair and make-up looked good. She had not worn any make-up in years. She even dusted off her most precious dress out of the closet, which she had been saving for special occasions.

Conall was amazed. He thought, "Gosh, she is already transforming even before taking the potion." He gave her a glass of her favourite red wine.

For the first time in almost fifteen years, they discovered how to laugh once again and remembered why they fell in love in the first place.

As his recognition for his wife grew, she began to take better care of herself. Their home, which was once dark and gloomy, became spotlessly clean and full of fresh flowers. The walls which were once colored with a brownish grey tone, now repainted in light pastel colors.

One day Conall went home from a long, hard day at work. He took note of his wife and noticed that she had lost weight, her hair looked different, and she looked at least ten years younger. He looked at her with all the love, gratitude and passion of a newlywed and appreciatively said: "I love you, my beautiful wife."

Conall had not said those words in over ten years. Tears streamed down his wife's cheeks. They embraced and she looked at him tenderly and whispered, "I love you, too, you are back, my love."

Weeks went by when Maya went back to the kitchen with Ultan. Conall was there washing the dishes as always, but this time whistling a happy tune and he seemed to be glowing.

"Tell me, Conall. What happened?" asked Maya.

"The potion worked just like you said it would. Every day my wife became more beautiful. I thank you for the gift you have given us, I will never forget it."

Ultan looked at Maya.

Maya smiled and said: "Thank you, Conall, for sharing your story."

Ultan and Maya left the kitchen. She was beaming with joy.

"Any miracle can happen when someone truly believes," she whispered. "More importantly, it can happen when love, appreciation and gratitude are present."

"Ok, it works. How do we spread this to everyone?" asked the brother.

"What do you think?" replied Maya

"I am not sure if you are doing this because you truly care about others or you simply appreciate their roles in your life?" wondered Ultan.

"You've just given me a great idea, big brother! I normally thank eight to ten people every day. When I do that, I stop and pay attention to what they are saying and look them in the eyes and see them as a complete being, an equal. When I develop that connection, I make sure that they know the wonderful contribution they have made in my life."

"That's great, Maya. I never really thank people the way you do. I've never stopped to connect with them or to truly see the difference they have made in my life," Ultan confessed.

"Ok, it is time to see the bigger picture, big brother. You see, I do this with at least eight people every day. Those eight people usually interact with at least another eight people. So, indirectly, I am helping brighten the day of more than 500 people."

Maya was pleased. "But imagine this multiplying even more once people start getting into the habit of thanking and appreciating others. It is so easy to do. Just by telling someone that who they are makes a wonderful difference and who they are matters."

Ultan looked around every time people walked by. They all acknowledged Maya with huge, sincere smiles like she was a part of their family. Ultan was touched.

That day Ultan realised that creating a better world did not include war, money or politics. It just took one open heart with a beautiful idea.

THE END

OR MAYBE NOT JUST YET…

SEE NEXT PAGES

Check if any more Books in The Legends of Altai series is available

www.legendsofaltai.com

STUDENT, READER WORKBOOK

STORY: 1
The King and The Thief

What have you learned?
Write a few sentences about what this story teaches you.

_____

_____

_____

_____

_____

_____

_____

_____

_____

_____

_____

_____

My New Words

Write the definition for all of the words listed. Once this task is completed, write a phrase that contains the word.

Luxury

_____
_____
_____

Lavish

_____
_____
_____

Burden

_____
_____
_____

Flourish

_____
_____
_____

To judge

_____
_____
_____

Compassion

_____
_____
_____

Selfishness

_____
_____
_____

ACTIVITIES – MY EXPEREINCE

Joining a New Group

Did you like this activity? Why or why not?

_____
_____
_____

_____

_____

_____

_____

_____

What was easy about it and what was hard?

_____

_____

_____

_____

_____

_____

_____

Class Debate

Can you remember any points that were made for and against this story? What did you think?

_____

_____

_____

_____

_____

Outside Visit

Where did you go? What did you do?

_____

_____

_____

_____

_____

_____

_____

_____

_____

_____

_____

_____

_____

_____

_____

_____

_____

Role Play

Did the story change when you acted it out? In what ways?

_____
_____
_____
_____
_____
_____
_____
_____
_____
_____
_____
_____
_____
_____
_____
_____
_____

Writing Activity

What help did you ask King Argoz for?

_____
_____
_____
_____

A Few Questions

How does this story make you feel? Why?

_____
_____
_____
_____

What is the part you like most? Why?

_____
_____
_____
_____

What is the part that you like the least? Why?

_____

_____
_____
_____

How could the lesson learned in this Story affect and benefit your life?

_____
_____
_____
_____

What is a simple action, behaviour that you could implement straight away in your life?

_____
_____
_____
_____

Describe how this lesson could be used to benefit your relationships with others and study:

_____
_____
_____
_____

Describe how this lesson could be used to benefit your future:

_____
_____
_____
_____

Is there anyone in your life that is going through something similar to what is happening in the story?

_____
_____
_____
_____

STORY: 2
King Argoz and the Wisdom of the Blue Violet

Write a few sentences about what this story teaches you.

My New Words

Write the definition for all of the words listed. Once this task is completed, write a phrase that contains the word.

Astronomy

_____
_____
_____
_____

Serenity

_____
_____
_____
_____

Bountifulness

_____
_____
_____
_____

Purpose

_____

_____
_____

To inhale

_____
_____
_____

Celebration

_____
_____
_____

Activities - My Experience

Word Search
Some people enjoy this activity more than others. Are you one of them? Don't worry if you found it hard, we are all different.

_____

_____

_____

_____

_____

_____

_____

_____

Emotional Literacy Exercise
What was easy about this activity and what was hard and why?

_____

_____

_____

_____

_____

_____

_____

Art Work
What flower did you like the most? Why?

_____
_____
_____
_____
_____
_____
_____

Role Play
What do you remember most about the Role Play/Drama?

_____
_____
_____
_____
_____
_____
_____
_____
_____

A Few Questions

How does this story make you feel? Why?

_____
_____
_____

What is the part you like most? Why?

_____
_____
_____

What is the part that you like the least? Why?

_____
_____
_____
_____
_____

How could the lesson learned in this Story affect and benefit your life?

_____
_____
_____
_____

What is a simple action, behaviour that you could implement straight away in your life?

_____
_____
_____
_____

Describe how this lesson could be used to benefit your relationships with others and study:

_____
_____
_____
_____

Describe how this lesson could be used to benefit your future:

_____
_____
_____

Is there anyone in your life that is going through something similar to what is happening in the story?

_____
_____
_____
_____
_____
_____
_____

STORY: 3
King Argoz and the Street Girl

Write a few sentences about what this story teaches you.

My New Words

Write the definition for all of the words listed. Once this task is completed, write a phrase that contains the word.

Comradeship

_____
_____
_____

Camouflage

_____
_____
_____

To scavenge

_____
_____
_____

To patrol

_____
_____
_____

Beggar

_____
_____
_____

Wondrous

_____
_____
_____

Responsibility

_____
_____
_____

Reward

_____
_____
_____

Outside Visit

Write a few sentences about whom you saw and who you met

_____
_____
_____
_____

Practical Project

How are you going to change as a result of this activity?

_____
_____
_____
_____
_____
_____
_____
_____

Role Play

Did you enjoy this activity? Why or why not?

_____
_____
_____
_____
_____
_____

Story Board

What did you do towards creating the class storyboard? List out your actions

_____
_____
_____
_____
_____

Writing Activity

What feelings do you think Prince Ultan had when he knew that he was going to have a new adopted sister?

_____

_____

_____

_____

_____

_____

_____

_____

_____

_____

_____

_____

_____

_____

_____

Adoption Activity

What has the class decided to adopt? What will be your role in caring for it/them?

_____
_____
_____
_____
_____
_____
_____
_____
_____
_____
_____

A Few Questions

How does this story make you feel? Why?

_____
_____
_____

What is the part you like most? Why?

_____
_____
_____
_____

What is the part that you like the least? Why?

_____
_____
_____
_____

How could the lesson learned in this Story affect and benefit your life?

_____
_____
_____
_____
_____
_____
_____
_____

What is a simple action, behaviour that you could implement straight away in your life?

_____
_____
_____
_____

Describe how this lesson could be used to benefit your relationships with others and study:

_____
_____
_____
_____

Describe how this lesson could be used to benefit your future:

_____
_____
_____
_____

Is there anyone in your life that is going through something similar to what is happening in the story?

_____
_____
_____
_____

STORY: 4
Princess Maya's Plan

Write a few sentences about what this story teaches you.

My New Words

Write the definition for all of the words listed. Once this task is completed, write a phrase that contains the word.

Appreciate

_____
_____
_____
_____

Transform

_____
_____
_____
_____

Intrigue

Congratulate

Implement

Speechless

Placebo

___

Activities

Appreciation Exercise 1
How many people did you manage to appreciate and what did you say to them?

Appreciation Exercise 2

How many things can you appreciate in a single day? List them.

_____
_____
_____
_____
_____
_____
_____
_____
_____
_____
_____
_____
_____
_____
_____

Art Work

What inner qualities does Princess Maya possess?

_____
_____
_____

Craft Work

Did you enjoy this activity? Who did you give your Certificate of Appreciation to and why?

_____
_____
_____
_____
_____
_____

Writing Activity

Who did you invite and why?

_____
_____
_____
_____

How could the lesson learned in this Story affect and benefit your life?

_____
_____
_____
_____

A Few Questions

How does this story make you feel? Why?

_____
_____
_____
_____
_____

What is the part you like most? Why?

_____
_____
_____

What is the part that you like the least? Why?

_____
_____
_____

How could the lesson learned in this Story affect and benefit your life?

_____
_____
_____

What is a simple action, behaviour that you could implement straight away in your life?

_____
_____
_____

Describe how this lesson could be used to benefit your relationships with others and study:

_____
_____
_____
_____

Describe how this lesson could be used to benefit your future:

_____
_____
_____
_____

Is there anyone in your life that is going through something similar to what is happening in the story?

_____
_____
_____
_____

GALLERY OF ASSETS

PRINCESS MAYA'S WINDOW

COLOURING BOOK

King Argoz   Xavier the Wise

TEACHERS AND PARENTS WORK BOOK

Introduction

This handbook is a guide to the first book in the Legends of Altai book series.

As a teacher, you have the opportunity of being able to encourage a young mind to develop value and respect for all life. These stories have been written to showcase life values and the greatness of life potential to children.

It is hoped that this book will help you as a teacher to open the eyes of your students to the wonders of nature – the majesty of the seas, the puzzles of the heavens, the complexities of human emotions – in all their myriad forms. In fact, feelings and empathetic re-creation of feelings form the basis of most of the exercises in this handbook.

If you are a using this book as a parent, then it's worth remembering that none of us was given a manual at the start of our parenthood, and so most of us struggle along trying to survive as best we can. Some of the exercises are not applicable to very small groups, but those that most suitable are marked with this symbol . Another very powerful way to use the guide is to prompt discussions between yourself and your child or children.

If you are using this book in a classroom setting, you may wish to incorporate the exercises into your own lesson plan. Ideas for lesson plans are given with each tale, along with a summary of the main point/wisdom lesson. Some of the exercises may be carried out of the school into the broader society. This is because one of the great messages of the stories is that we live in an interconnected world, and that what happens to one part of the world happens to all of it.

The most important thing, wither in the classroom or at home, is to create an atmosphere of trust and acceptance. Plan the time carefully but allow for spontaneity as well.

Perhaps the greatest gift we can give children is to empower their imagination. We are born with a rich inner world which in the past has often been crushed by overly rigid systems of tuition and discipline. But the inner life is a great resource which, if properly encouraged and trained, will feed a person's spirit for a whole lifetime.

The stories have a personal slant in that I believe that divine presence is in all beings. However, we live a diverse society with a great range of religions and so references to God have been made more neutral – as The Great One. The aim is always to teach without preaching, and to show without prescribing.

Although the Workbook is aimed at children, it is relevant to us all.

You might want to Award the Diploma (Template in Appendix) to each child as a final touch to round off the experience of reading the book.

Please enjoy the Tales and any feedback is welcomed.

How to Use this Book

For Teachers

How you use this guide and the stories depends on your understanding of your students. Another important factor is the age of the students themselves and also their grasp of the English language.

If the students do not speak English as their first language, or if you are using the stories in an ESL context, then you may wish to use some of the vocabulary, language activities first before moving onto the life lessons/wisdom aspects of each story. There is a useful list of questions which you can use to initiate discussions or set essay topics in Appendix 1.

Suggestions are given for activities which will focus the student's enjoyment of the story, leading to an understanding and internalisation of the life lessons and wisdom contained each one of them. You may wish to adapt the activities according the age and abilities of the class.

For Parents

How you use this guide will depend on the age of your child/children. You may want to re-enforce new vocabulary and spelling as a lead-in to the story, or you may want to just read the story to them and ask them what they have understood by listening to it. There is a useful list of questions which you can use to initiate discussions in Appendix 1

One way to integrate the life lesson/wisdom is to relate it to everyday experience. For example, if someone has judged another person recently and not shown compassion, you could ask your child how things could be different if peoples' attitudes changed.

The important thing to remember is that you can't get it wrong as long as you keep an open channel of dialogue between yourself and your child. Reflect on the lessons for yourself and be prepared to change your own mind!

STORY 1

The King and The Thief

Summary of the Life lesson/Wisdom

You can't judge another until you are in their shoes (living their lives, experiencing their struggle). Once you truly realize why they are the way you are, how they have come to certain life conclusions, compassion can replace what once was harsh judgment.

Lesson Plan

The Native Americans have a saying: 'Do not judge me until you have walked in my moccasins'. Write this on the board and ask he children what they think it means. Be prepared to explain that moccasins were the shoes of the Native Americans.

Pre-teach vocabulary and ask students to note it in their books.

Read the story to the students.

Ask the students what they think it means and guide them towards the summary of the life lesson – and maybe other points they will see in the story.

Ask the students to do some of the activities.

Ask the students to reflect on people they dislike. It is quite challenging for students to come out with people they dislike that are actually present, so it might be an idea for them to describe other people. You could set the scene by talking about a person you didn't like but came to understand better by understanding their circumstances.

Pre-teach Vocabulary

Luxury, lavish, burden, flourish, pay taxes, compassion, selfishness, to judge,

Activities

Joining a New Group

Form three or four groups in the class eg penguins, lions, ravens, crocodiles etc. There should be at least four people in each group. Now ask one student in each group to try to join another group eg one 'penguin' tries to become a 'lion'. The group has to interview the new applicant and decide whether to accept them or not. Do this several times, so that each person has the experience of having to change groups.

It is important with this activity to allow students to talk about their experience. For example, 'It was hard for me, as a crocodile, to join the ravens. I had to convince them that I wouldn't hurt them'.

Use the experience to reflect on pre-judging things and people and the power that labelling has. Broaden the discussion from animal characteristics to human life choices if appropriate.

Class Debate

Set up a debate with speakers for and against the proposition. Establish the ground rules for debating first eg polite behaviour, no personalisation and no name-calling.

Proposition 1: This House believes that you cannot judge another person until you have walked in their shoes.

Proposition 2: This House believes that you have the right to live in luxury while others starve.

Outside Visit

Arrange a visit to homeless people in order to donate food, used clothing, toiletries.

Role Play

Ask the students to act out the story in small groups. Allow students to improvise as they go.

Younger children might enjoy making props for older ones eg papier mache vegetables and fruit.

Writing Activity

Write a letter to King Argoz asking for help in a difficult situation. You might want to go over the basics of letter writing with the class first.

STORY 2

King Argoz and the Wisdom of the Blue Violet

Summary of the Life lesson/Wisdom

Accepting who we are can make our life full of great potential instead of sorrow. Look at the advantages that you as person have instead of focusing on the limitations. Stat to see the glass as half full rather than half empty.

Lesson Plan

Start by drawing a glass on the whiteboard half full of water. Ask the class whether it is half full or half empty. Ask the class whether those things mean the same thing.

Write the following on the board *Kng rgz nd th wsdm f th bl vlt*. Be prepared to explain that the vowels are missing – can the children guess them. This little exercise stretches the mind and encourages people to think beyond the limitations of a situation.

Pre-teach vocabulary and ask students to note it in their books.

Read out the title of the story and ask the students to guess what the story is about. What is a blue violet? Can it exist? Stretch their minds.

Read the story – or ask the class to read paragraphs of it in turn.

Ask the students to do some of the activities.

Ask the students to reflect on what limits people. You might want to open up the subject of differently abled people here, or just different gifts around the class. You could round off the lesson by doing a mingle exercise in which students go around the room telling other students what their gift is.

Pre-teach Vocabulary

Astronomy, serenity, bountifulness, purpose, to inhale, celebration

Activities

Word Search

Use the wordsearch below or use a Word Search program (easily available on the internet, try http://puzzlemaker.discoveryeducation.com/) to generate new words or words that children have difficulty spelling. They then have to find the letters in a jumble and this helps their minds focus on the actual letters.

Emotional Literacy Exercise

Write the words SAD ANGRY FRIGHTENED JOYFUL on the board and ask the children to explain what each word means. Ask them to give an instance of when they feel this in their lives.

This would be a good lead-in to the role play – as each flower is associated with a specific emotion.

Art Work

Draw the flowers on the board or ask the children to make drawings themselves. Display the drawings on a class board. If time permits, you could make large-scale cardboard representations of the flowers, which could be carried by the children as they do the role play.

Role Play

There are several ways to do this role play – one way would be to start in the garden with the flowers talking amongst themselves.

Let the flowers talk amongst themselves and express their emotions. Encourage a dialogue between them. 'Why are you sad/frightened etc? What can help you overcome that feeling?'

STORY 3

King Argoz and the Street Girl

Summary of the Life lesson/Wisdom

Everyone is important; no one should be left behind, no matter how they look, or how poor they are. Everyone matters. We are all responsible for the outside reality we live in, we are all interconnected. When judgment fades and love and compassion surface, anything is possible. Unity brings strength, separation brings weakness and failure.

Lesson Plan

The lesson focuses on seeing things as they really are, and seeing through our own judgements. There

Pre-teach vocabulary and ask students to note it in their books.

Tell the children the title of the story and ask them to predict what the life lesson will be. Teach the children a skim reading technique. Ask them to read the story very fast and tell you the main points. Then read it again for the details.

Ask the students to do some of the activities.

You could round off the lesson by talking about the power of adoption. Some of the children may be adopted, how does this feel.

Pre-teach Vocabulary

Comradeship, camouflage, to scavenge, to patrol, beggar, wondrous, responsibility, reward

Activities

Outside Visit

Arrange a visit to a food outlet where street people are given food and clothing. Make sure that you allow plenty of time to discuss and process the visit.

Practical Project

Encourage the children to think of ways they could help homeless people – eg collecting items that they don't need eg used clothing, unopened food packages. You might want to tie this in to a campaign that one of the charities in your locality.

Role Play

Get the children to act out the story. As an added twist you could start with Maya, from the time that she was abandoned in the market. Then bring in the disguised king. Changing the focus makes Maya the centre of the story.

Story Board

Divide the children into groups of three or four. Give each group a story board and ask them to tell the story in words and pictures. It's a good idea to blow the story board up to A3 size so the children have plenty of room. It's also an idea to cut out drawing rectangles so that some children can be working on the drawings while others in the group are preparing the written work.

Writing Activity

Write a letter from Prince Ultan to his new sister Maya, welcoming her into the family.

Adoption Activity

Many things are adopted in life eg dogs, cats, orphans in developing countries, second hand clothes, trees. Encourage the class to adopt something simple eg a plant, which can then be taken care of as a community responsibility.

STORY 4

Princess Maya's Plan

Summary of the Life lesson/Wisdom

What happens in your life is 90% attitude and 10% events. To change your life, change your attitudes, to change your attitudes, change your thinking. When people get recognition they do a better job. No matter who you are or what you do, you are part of the great matrix of life, you matter, your life and who you are makes a difference.

Lesson Plan

Lead in to the class by giving some words of appreciation to the children. You may like to draw attention to the 'unsung heroes' who don't normally get praise but who make life better for everyone.

Pre-teach vocabulary and ask students to note it in their books.

Tell the children the title of the story and ask them to predict what the life lesson will be. Ask them if they make plans.

Read the story – or ask the class to read paragraphs of it in turn.

Ask the students to do some of the activities.

Ask the students whether there's somebody they can give appreciation to when they go home.

Pre-teach Vocabulary

To appreciate, placebo, intrigue, congratulate, implement, speechless, transform

Activities

Appreciation Exercise 1

Ask the children to walk round the class and tell to as many people as possible that they appreciate them. Model this activity by participating as well.

Appreciation Exercise 2

Take the children outside and include nature as some of the things that can be appreciated eg trees, streams, flowers, sun, the rain etc.

Art Work

Ask the children to make a painting of Princess Maya – either individually or in small groups. Try to get them to express her inner beauty (generosity, insight, capacity to inspire others, seeing the best in other people etc) as well as her outer beauty.

Craft Work

Ask the children to make a Certificate of Appreciation for someone they know – it could be a parent, or relative, or a friend.

You might want to give them a template for this or some examples to work from. The Certificate should include the qualities that are most noteworthy in the child's eyes, so you may want to brainstorm a list of possibilities on the board eg kind, gentle, good cook, encouraging etc

Writing Activity

Ask the children to write to a celebrity and invite them to visit the school, if possible. If the celebrity is locally based this is more likely to be able to happen!

The letter should include the reasons for inviting the celebrity – why this person is inspirational.

Appendix 1:

Questions to ask about each story

How does this story make you feel? Why?

What is the part you like most? Why?

What is the part that you like the least? Why?

How could the lesson learned in this Story affect and benefit your life?

What is a simple action, behaviour that you could implement straight away in your life?

Describe how this lesson could be used to benefit your relationships:

Describe how this lesson could be used to benefit your study/work:

Describe how this lesson could be used to benefit your future:

Is there anyone in your life that is going through something similar to what is happening in the story?

Appendix 2:

GALLERY OF ASSETS

Appendix 3: Princess Maya's Window

Appendix 4: Certificate of Achievement

SHARE THE MESSAGE

These stories changed my life as a child and continue to do so every day. Every time I read or reflect upon them, I find a new message or a layer of meaning. I would love to hear about the impact these tales have had in your lives. Have they changed a hard situation? Did they inspire you to make a stand? Perhaps, they have simply touched you and reminded you of the important things in life.

I welcome you to share your testimonials with me and would be honoured to hear what you have to say. If you have a personal story you believe could fit in the series, please let me know. I always welcome the gift of wisdom and any opportunity to share it. You may contact me at:

www.legendsofaltai.com/pages/share.php

KEEPING IN TOUCH

- If you are interested in future books, please join our **mailing list** by visiting: www.legendsofaltai.com/pages/keep-in-touch.php

- Visit the official *Legends of Altai* **website** : www.legendsofaltai.com and bookmark it for future reference.

YOU CAN MAKE A DIFFERENCE!

You can play an important role in fanning the winds of change around the globe. You have the power to start this change within your own family, neighbourhood, city, state, country and the world. It all starts with you. It continues by letting others know what you've discovered. Let's start a revolution of self-discovery!

I truly hope to create a lasting ritual of bedtime stories that contain wisdom and inspiration. If we give just a little more, our world will see many amazing moments from simple small gestures.

It can start with you...

Spreading the word is easy and free. It can be an incredible rewarding experience.

Below are some of the few things you could do to truly make a difference in someone life, school, community and state.

- Share a **free chapter** with your friends: Chapter 7: "King Ultan and his 3 Sons" can be downloaded to share: www.legendsofaltai.com/pages/free-gifts.php

- A good way to spread this message is to ask your **local school & library** to obtain this book and/or the rest of the series.

- Couldn't find a copy of this book at your **local book-store**? Then ask about it! Most book-stores will order copies if requested.

- If you are part of a **book club**, please mention how this book has inspired you.

- Give the book as a Birthday or Christmas present.

- Speak with your school Principal or teachers in regards to making this book part of the **curriculum or school library**.

- Use the book bulk discount (on the site) and offer the book as a **Fund-Raising** product. (Under the Bookstores, Schools & Libraries link on the site)

- Write a **blog, articles** about your experience with the Legends of Altai and submit it to your web site or local newspaper.

- Let your friends and family know about the Lewgends of Altai through your **Facebook**

- Let your friends and family know about the Lewgends of Altai through your **Twitter**

ANY HELP IN SPREADING THE WORD ABOUT THIS BOOK IS APPRECIATED!

I wish you all the very best your mind and heart can conceive.
Paolo F. Tiberi

WHOLESALE & PRIVATE LABEL EDITIONS

Buy in bulk/wholesale for your fund-raiser, institution, school (Workbook for Students and Teacher Reference Book also Available)

For more information visit:
www.legendsofaltai.com/pages/bookstores_libraries.php

Arrange a "Special Edition – Private Label" of this book for your company, organisation, or association with your own personalised message.
(Minimum orders apply.)
www.legendsofaltai.com/pages/contact.php

Book the Author for an Event

Paolo F. Tiberi is a successful entrepreneur, published author, public speaker, educator and motivator. He was invited to speak at several television shows in Italy and had his own program in a small regional television channel in Rome before deciding to move to Australia.

There, he was invited to speak and inspire the unemployed people at the Salvation Army Employment Plus and had a 30-minute segment on Radio Italia, an Italian radio station broadcasting to 250,000 Australia wide.

To read the inspirational full life story of Paolo visit:

http://www.paolotiberi.com/pages/paolo_tiberi.html

Special Thanks

The best creative processes use great minds to make a work not only stand out, but stand apart. This book, with its precious stories, has been developed by ancient parables. Many of these stories are hundreds, even thousands, of years old. English is not my mother tongue, so my beautiful wife, Abigail Tiberi, has been so gracious to help make the stories more interesting and rich, using much of her free time to support this project. She also assisted in modifying my English whenever necessary.

A very special thanks also goes to all the devoted individuals who have helped editing and proof reading the stories in this book. These individuals are Ramona Resurreccion, Margaret Preller Osako, Megan Peterson Morrow and Jillian McKellan, they have been of great assistance in regards to the readability of what you hold in your hands today.

The front cover mountain ranges has been modified from a picture taken by Ondrej Žvácek. The castle in the distance is a modified version of Kishi Church taken by Matthias Kabel. I thank all of them for taking those pictures.

I offer my fondest thanks to all the teachers, people, places and events that have made me the person I am today. They have all given me a little more wisdom than I would have otherwise not have experienced. Each day I discover more, I learn more and realize that I still have much more to learn. Knowledge is a lifetime quest that I embrace with a passion.

And a final and most appreciative thank you goes to <u>YOU the reader</u>, for having invested in this book. I am thankful that you are taking the time to enjoy the stories and the knowledge and wisdom they contain.

NOTES

NOTES

NOTES

NOTES

NOTES

www.ingramcontent.com/pod-product-compliance
Lightning Source LLC
LaVergne TN
LVHW051835080426
835512LV00018B/2897

LEGENDS OF ALTAI
BOOK I

I welcome you to the beautiful realm of 'The Legends of Altai'. This is a storytelling book that opens both the heart and mind of its readers. It aims to bridge a connection between life, understanding our relationship with others, knowing our purpose and finding a sense of inner peace.

The stories in the Legends of Altai are told in a very easy to follow format that are appropriate for all ages. They contain an inspiring combination of philosophy, ancient wisdom, and storytelling. They are presented in a completely accessible way that makes even the most profound concepts easily understood.

While the stories are geared for children aged 5-12+, parents and other adults alike have found the tales most uplifting, beneficial and applicable to their own lives. I truly hope that the messages in this book will reveal themselves to you and your child in many different ways and on many different levels as experienced by many others.

"I cannot tell you what a joy it has been to get this series of books into my home. As a loving mom and author I am always looking for books that entertain, educate, and open up opportunities for conversations with my daughter. The Legends of Altai series does just that. Every tale in the book takes you away to a story that is amazing and thoughtful. This one is a must for every child's collection and adults too!"
Jill McKellan author of 'Brophey's Forest Adventures'

"These beautifully crafted and uplifting stories are deceptively simple, but contain deep wisdom. A must have book for all the children in your life and also for the child within you."
Frances Wilks author of 'Intelligent Emotion'

"An inspiring book that has the power to help children become better, wiser, more compassionate human beings."
Glenn Adams - Public Speaker, Business Coach to Mercedes-Benz, BMW, Kenworth amongst others, but more importanlty, father of three.

Published by: Effective Life Strategies
www.effectivelifestrategies.com

www.legendsofaltai.com